Shaolin Monks

by Tony Smith

BELLWETHER MEDIA · MINNEAPOLIS, MN

TM

Are you ready to take it to the extreme?
Torque books thrust you into the action-packed world
of sports, vehicles, mystery, and adventure. These books
may include dirt, smoke, fire, and dangerous stunts.
Warning: read at your own risk.

Library of Congress Cataloging-in-Publication Data

Smith, Tony.
 Shaolin monks / by Tony Smith.
    p. cm. -- (Torque: History's greatest warriors)
 Includes bibliographical references and index.
 Summary: "Engaging images accompany information about Shaolin monks. The combination of
high-interest subject matter and light text is intended for students in grades 3 through 7"--Provided by
publisher.
 Audience: Grades 3-7.
 ISBN 978-1-60014-748-7 (hbk. : alk. paper)
 1. Kung Fu--History--Juvenile literature. 2. Shao lin si (Dengfeng Xian, China)--Juvenile literature. I.
Title.
 GV1114.7.S54155 2012
 796.815'9--dc23   2011029090

This edition first published in 2012 by Bellwether Media, Inc.

Printed in the United States of America, North Mankato, MN.

010112   1202

Contents

Who Are Shaolin Monks? 4

Shaolin Monk Training 8

Shaolin Monk Equipment... 12

Shaolin Monks Today 18

Glossary 22

To Learn More 23

Index 24

Who Are Shaolin Monks?

The Shaolin **Monastery** in China has stood for more than 1,500 years. Its monks are among the most famous fighters in the world.

Shaolin monks are followers of **Buddhism**. They believe in peace and nonviolence. However, they have fought when they felt their way of life was threatened. Their intense physical training and **discipline** make them fearsome warriors.

In 464 CE, an Indian-born Buddhist named Batuo came to China. Years later, he started the Shaolin Monastery. He believed that practicing self-discipline, tolerating pain, and mastering **martial arts** helped people grow spiritually. He taught his monks these skills. This made them excellent warriors. Monks have trained there ever since.

Shaolin Fact

In the mid-1500s, Shaolin monks fought several battles against Japanese pirates.

Shaolin Monastery

少林寺

Shaolin Monk Training

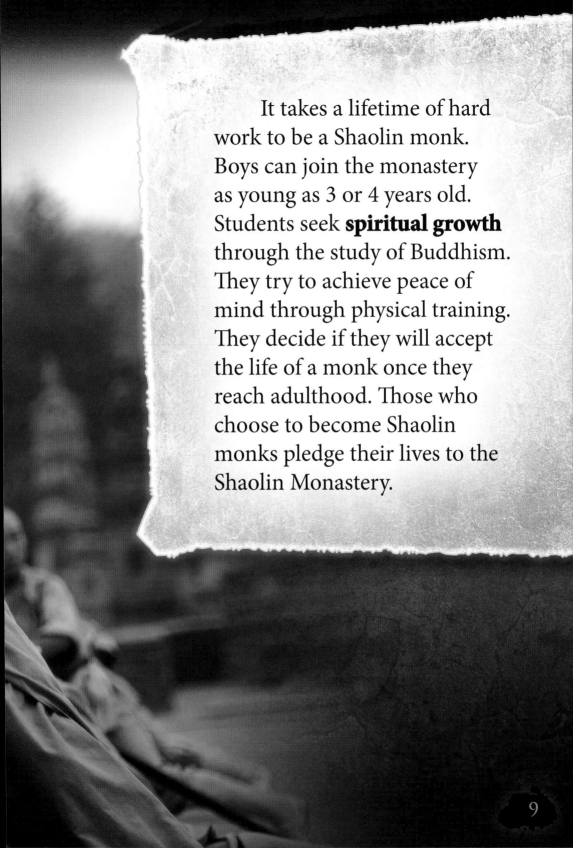

It takes a lifetime of hard work to be a Shaolin monk. Boys can join the monastery as young as 3 or 4 years old. Students seek **spiritual growth** through the study of Buddhism. They try to achieve peace of mind through physical training. They decide if they will accept the life of a monk once they reach adulthood. Those who choose to become Shaolin monks pledge their lives to the Shaolin Monastery.

Shaolin monks begin as **novices**. They do hard physical labor and practice Shaolin **kung fu**. Monks learn to fight with their hands and many different weapons. They learn to endure great physical pain. Shaolin monks must prove their skills in a series of tests. Those who pass all of the tests become **masters**. This often takes decades.

Shaolin Fact

Shaolin monks learn to master their *qi*, or energy flow. This gives them the power to break bricks with their hands and lie on a bed of spears without getting injured.

Shaolin Monk Equipment

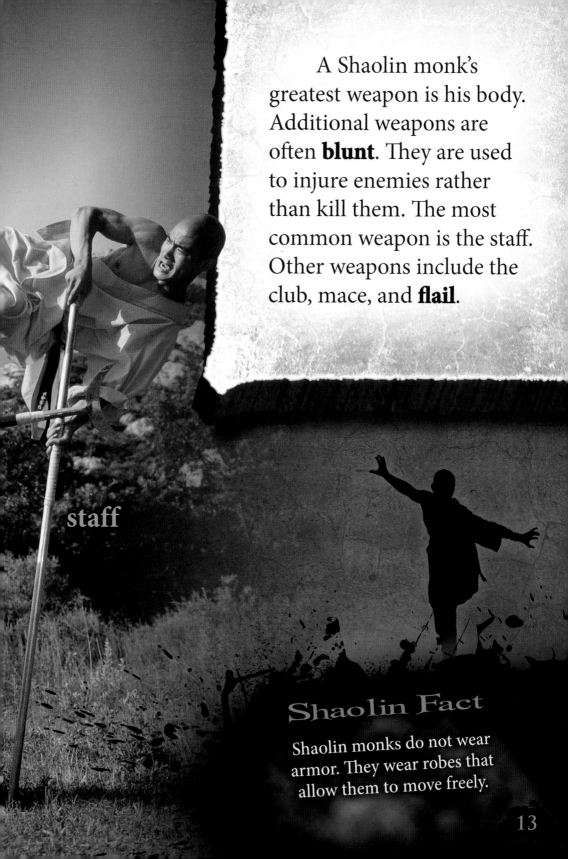

A Shaolin monk's greatest weapon is his body. Additional weapons are often **blunt**. They are used to injure enemies rather than kill them. The most common weapon is the staff. Other weapons include the club, mace, and **flail**.

staff

Shaolin Fact

Shaolin monks do not wear armor. They wear robes that allow them to move freely.

Shaolin monks also master the use of bladed weapons. These include the spear, sword, and **twin hooks**. Other common weapons include whips, ropes, and chains. Shaolin monks can even fight effectively with everyday objects such as shovels and rakes.

twin hooks

Shaolin Fact

Shaolin monks prefer close combat. They believe long-range weapons are dishonorable.

Kung Fu Styles

Shaolin monks learned to fight by watching animals fight. They developed different styles of kung fu that they named for different animals. Below are five styles that are common today.

 ### Tiger

The Tiger style is an all-out attack style. It often focuses on striking the opponent's throat.

 ### Dragon

Energy is the key to the Dragon style. Deep breathing and circular motions allow fighters to turn energy into powerful strikes.

 ### Crane

The Crane style focuses on patience and defense. The strategy is to let the opponent make the first move and to react to any mistakes.

 ### Snake

The Snake style emphasizes wisdom. The strategy is to capture and control the enemy. The Snake style uses very little violence.

Leopard

The Leopard style focuses on dodging enemy attacks and countering with lightning-quick strikes. It does not include any blocks.

Shaolin Monks Today

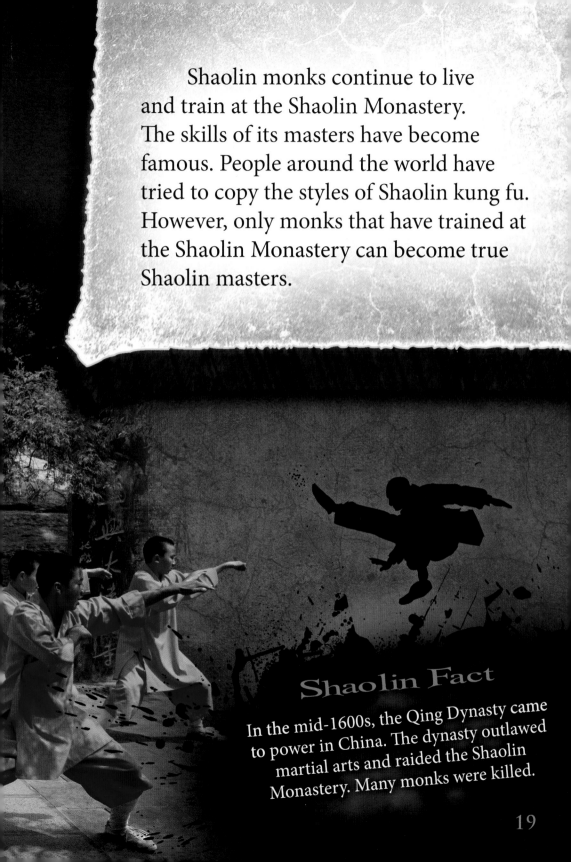

Shaolin monks continue to live and train at the Shaolin Monastery. The skills of its masters have become famous. People around the world have tried to copy the styles of Shaolin kung fu. However, only monks that have trained at the Shaolin Monastery can become true Shaolin masters.

Shaolin Fact

In the mid-1600s, the Qing Dynasty came to power in China. The dynasty outlawed martial arts and raided the Shaolin Monastery. Many monks were killed.

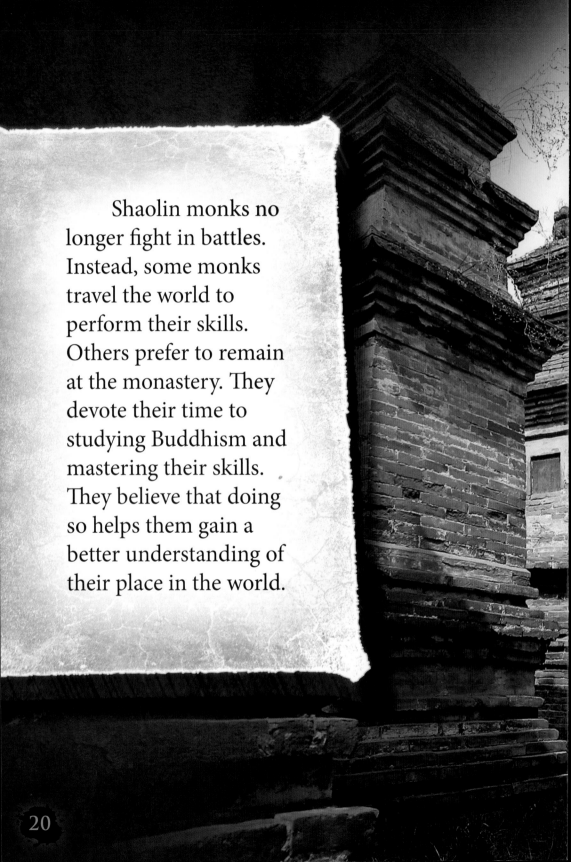

Shaolin monks no longer fight in battles. Instead, some monks travel the world to perform their skills. Others prefer to remain at the monastery. They devote their time to studying Buddhism and mastering their skills. They believe that doing so helps them gain a better understanding of their place in the world.

Glossary

blunt—not sharp

Buddhism—a religion that follows the teachings of Buddha; Buddhists value nonviolence, compassion, and self-control.

discipline—order and self-control

flail—a blunt weapon that is made up of a heavy ball connected to a handle by a chain

kung fu—a Chinese martial art; there are many different styles of kung fu.

martial arts—styles of fighting and self-defense that involve precise body movements

masters—monks who have passed certain tests to prove their skill in kung fu; it can take a monk decades to become a master.

monastery—a building where monks live together

novices—beginners; all Shaolin monks start as novices.

spiritual growth—the act of coming to a greater understanding of life and one's place in the universe

twin hooks—a pair of bladed weapons that have hooks on one end; twin hooks are used to slash and disarm enemies.

To Learn More

AT THE LIBRARY

Cooper, Alison. *Facts About Buddhism*. New York, N.Y.:
Rosen Pub.'s Rosen Central, 2011.

Liow, Kah Joon. *Shaolin: Legends of Zen and Kung Fu*.
Quebec, Canada: SilkRoad Networks Inc., 2006.

O'Shei, Tim. *Kung Fu*. Mankato, Minn.: Capstone Press, 2009.

ON THE WEB

Learning more about Shaolin monks
is as easy as 1, 2, 3.

1. Go to www.factsurfer.com.

2. Enter "Shaolin monks" into the search box.

3. Click the "Surf" button and you will see a list of
related Web sites.

With factsurfer.com, finding more information
is just a click away.

Index

armor, 13
Batuo, 6
Buddhism, 5, 6, 9, 20
China, 5, 6, 19
clothing, 13
discipline, 5, 6
energy, 10, 16
Japanese pirates, 6
kung fu, 10, 16, 17, 19
martial arts, 6, 19
masters, 10, 19
novices, 10
pain, 6, 10
qi, 10
Qing Dynasty, 19
Shaolin Monastery, 5, 6, 7, 9,
   19, 20
spiritual growth, 6, 9, 20
training, 5, 6, 9, 10, 14, 19
weapons, 10, 13, 14, 15

Great care has been taken to select images that are both historically accurate and engaging. The depictions of the warriors in this book may vary slightly due to the use of images from multiple sources and reenactments.